THE MINNESOTA VIKINGS

BY KIERAN DOWNS

EPIC

BELLWETHER MEDIA ★ MINNEAPOLIS, MN

EPIC BOOKS are no ordinary books. They burst with intense action, high-speed heroics, and shadows of the unknown. Are you ready for an Epic adventure?

This book is intended for educational use. Organization and franchise logos are trademarks of the National Football League (NFL). This is not an official book of the NFL. It is not approved by or connected with the NFL.

This edition first published in 2024 by Bellwether Media, Inc.

Library of Congress Cataloging-in-Publication Data

Names: Downs, Kieran, author.
Title: The Minnesota Vikings / by Kieran Downs.
Description: Minneapolis, MN : Bellwether Media, 2024. | Series: EPIC. NFL team profiles | Includes bibliographical references and index. | Audience: Ages 7-12 | Audience: Grades 2-3 | Summary: "Engaging images accompany information about the Minnesota Vikings. The combination of high-interest subject matter and light text is intended for students in grades 2 through 7"-- Provided by publisher.
Identifiers: LCCN 2023021954 (print) | LCCN 2023021955 (ebook) | ISBN 9798886874860 (library binding) | ISBN 9798886876741 (ebook)
Subjects: LCSH: Minnesota Vikings (Football team)--History--Juvenile literature.
Classification: LCC GV956.M5 D68 2024 (print) | LCC GV956.M5 (ebook) | DDC 796.332/6409776579--dc23/eng/20230515
LC record available at https://lccn.loc.gov/2023021954
LC ebook record available at https://lccn.loc.gov/2023021955

Editor: Betsy Rathburn Designer: Gabriel Hilger

Printed in the United States of America, North Mankato, MN.

TABLE OF CONTENTS

THE MINNEAPOLIS MIRACLE

CASE KEENUM

The Vikings face the Saints in the **playoffs**. With 10 seconds left, the Vikings are down by 1 point.

Vikings **quarterback** Case Keenum throws a pass. **Wide receiver** Stefon Diggs catches it. Diggs scores! The Vikings win!

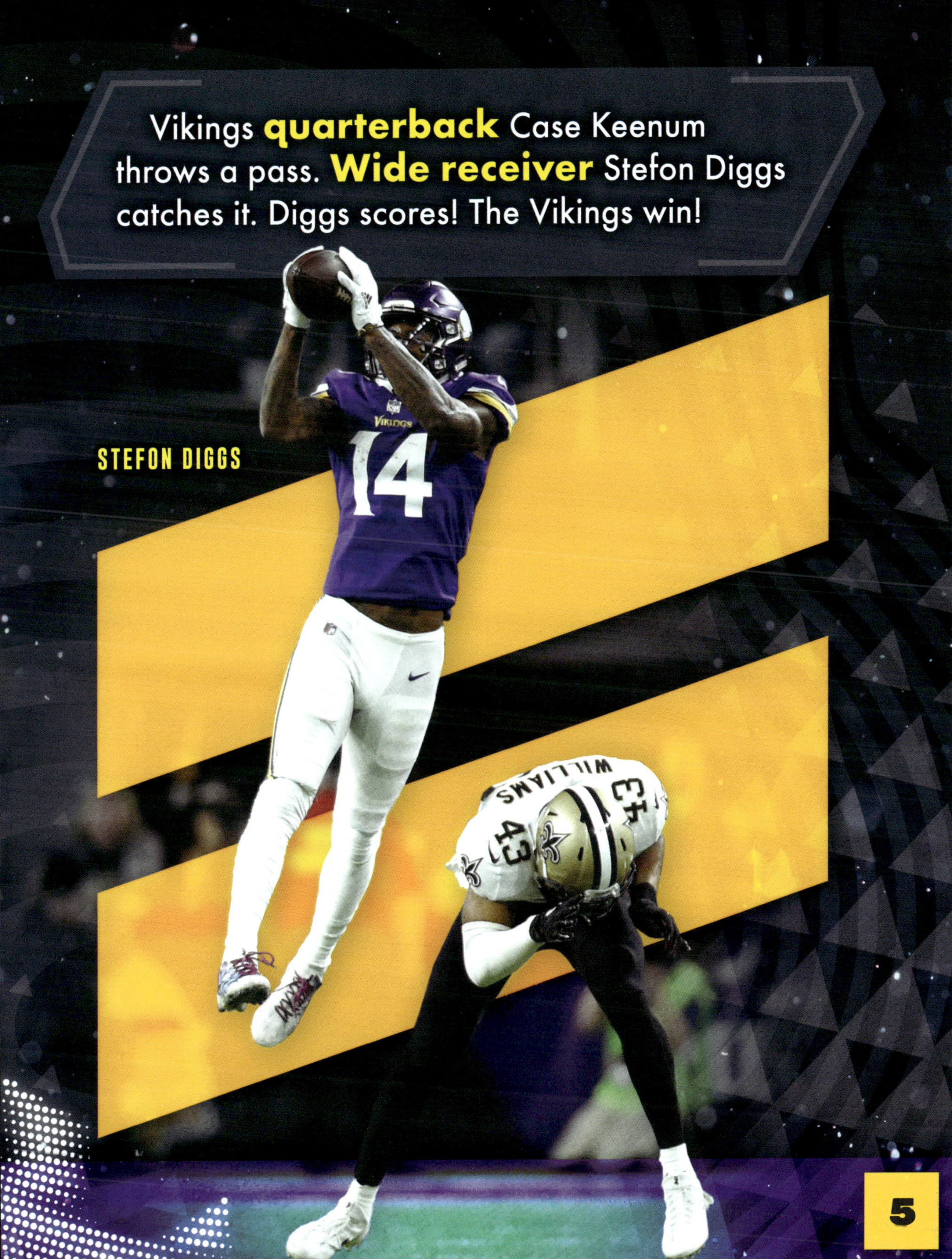

STEFON DIGGS

THE HISTORY OF THE VIKINGS

The Vikings joined the National Football League (NFL) in 1961. The team was not successful right away.

In 1967, **defensive tackle** Alan Page joined the team. He helped them start winning.

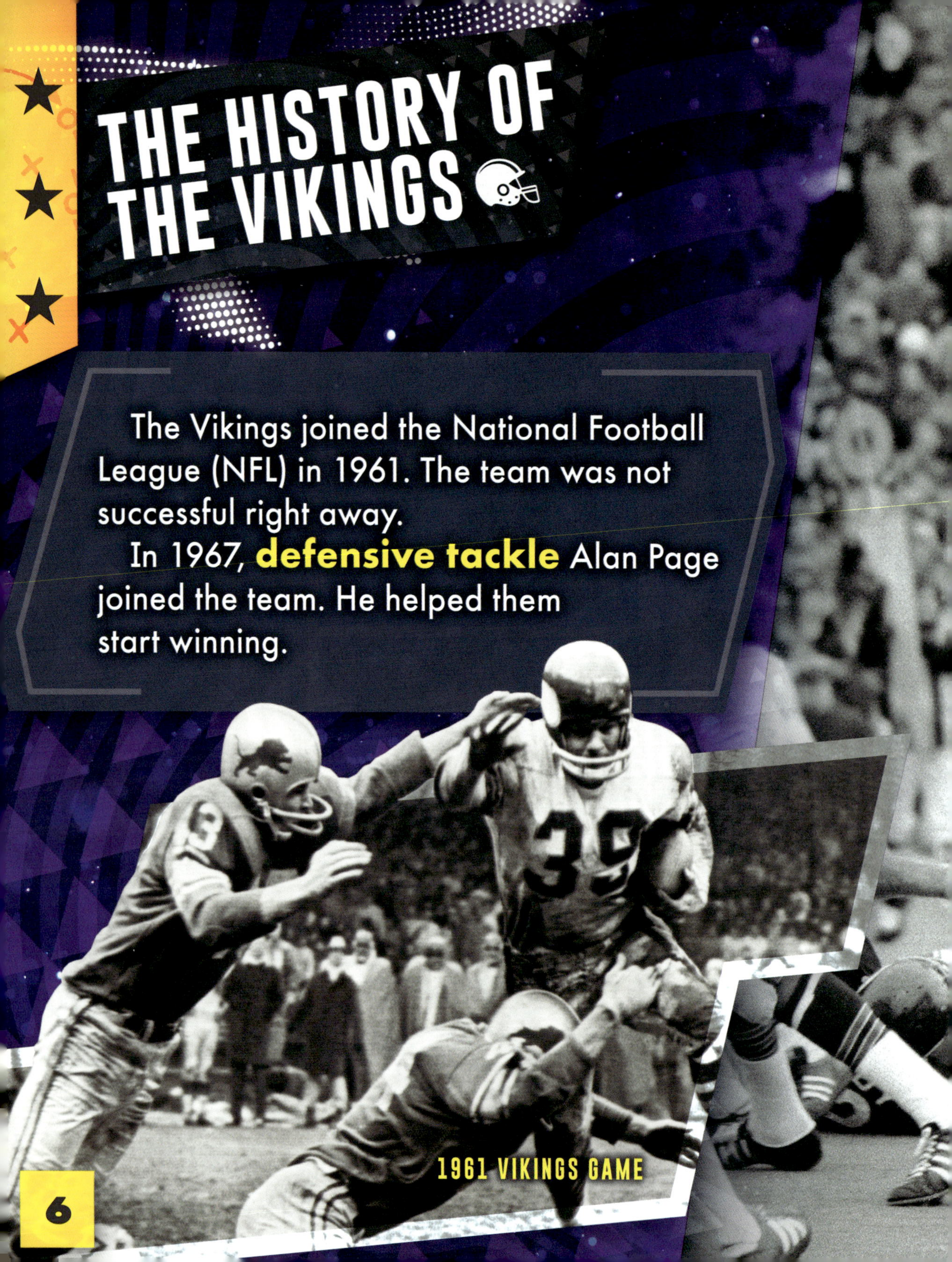

1961 VIKINGS GAME

ALAN PAGE

The Vikings won the NFL **championship** for the 1969 season. They were led by coach Bud Grant. But they lost in the **Super Bowl**.

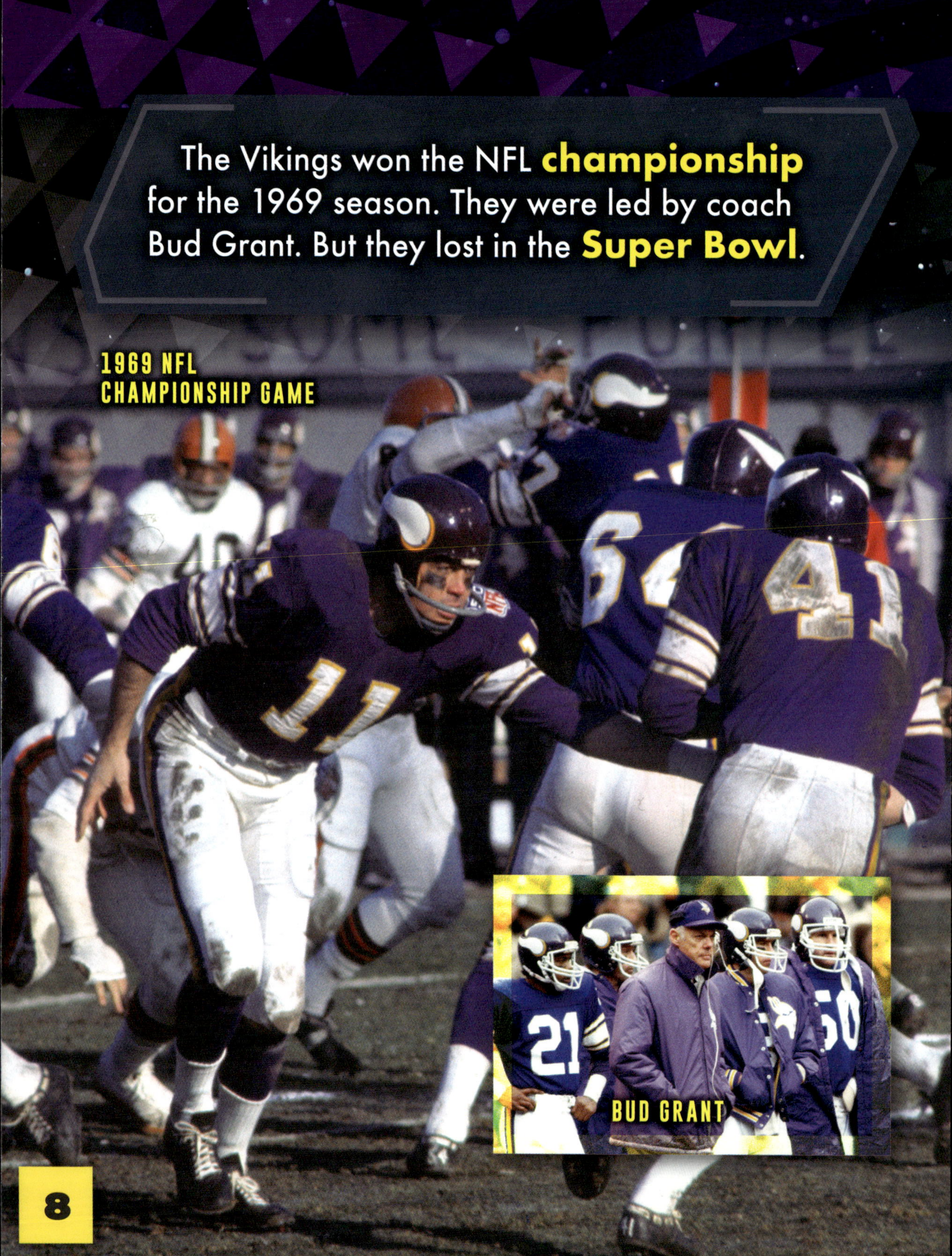

1969 NFL CHAMPIONSHIP GAME

BUD GRANT

LONGTIME COACH

Bud Grant coached more seasons than any other Vikings coach.

The Vikings played in three more Super Bowls in the 1970s. But they lost them all.

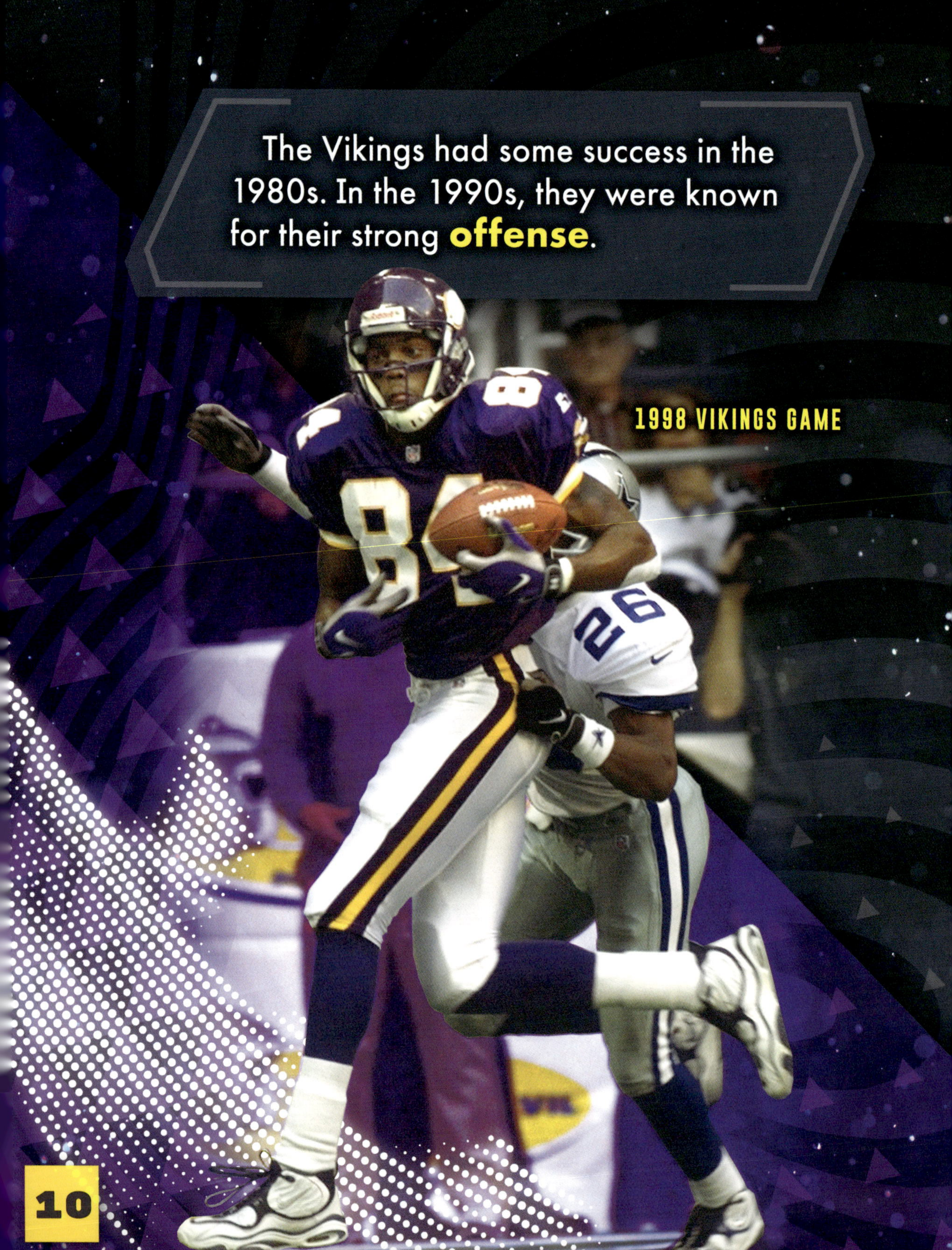

The Vikings had some success in the 1980s. In the 1990s, they were known for their strong **offense**.

1998 VIKINGS GAME

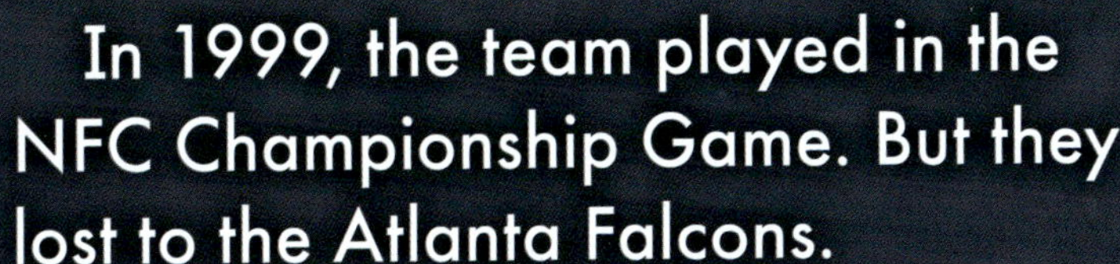

In 1999, the team played in the NFC Championship Game. But they lost to the Atlanta Falcons.

TROPHY CASE

NFC CENTRAL championships
14

NFC NORTH championships
5

NFC championships
3

NFL championship
1

The Vikings were a strong running team in the 2000s. In the 2010s, they reached the playoffs four times.

2009 VIKINGS GAME

In 2020, wide receiver Justin Jefferson joined the team. He helped the team win their **division** in 2022.

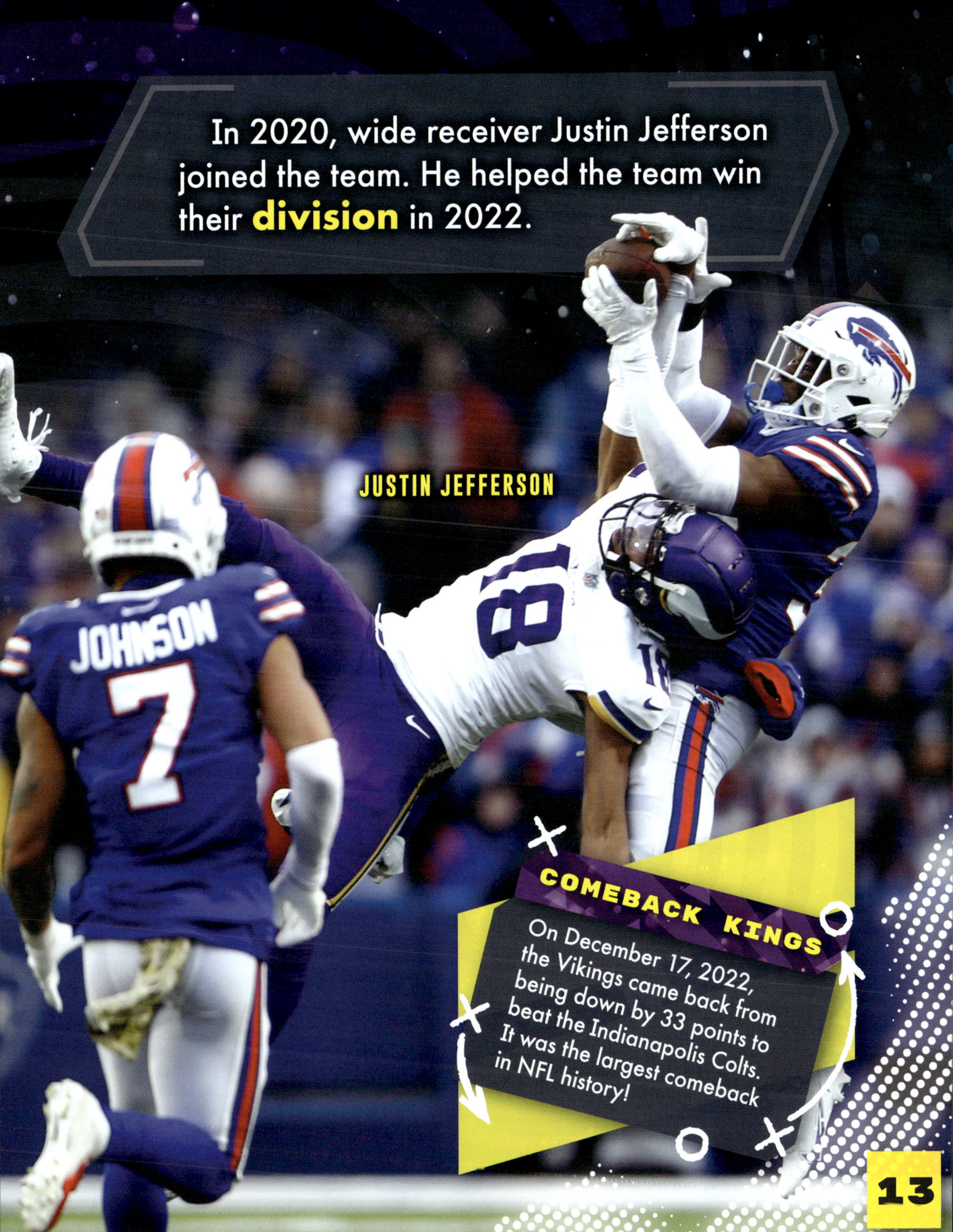

JUSTIN JEFFERSON

COMEBACK KINGS

On December 17, 2022, the Vikings came back from being down by 33 points to beat the Indianapolis Colts. It was the largest comeback in NFL history!

THE VIKINGS TODAY

The Vikings play home games in U.S. Bank **Stadium**. It is in Minneapolis, Minnesota.

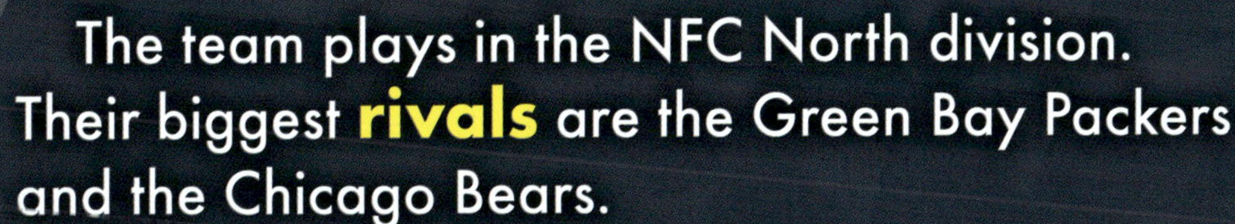

The team plays in the NFC North division. Their biggest **rivals** are the Green Bay Packers and the Chicago Bears.

LOCATION

MINNESOTA

U.S. BANK STADIUM

Minneapolis, Minnesota

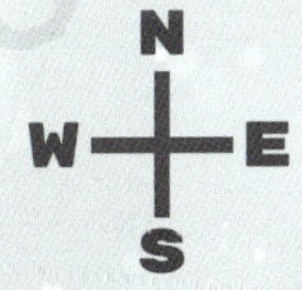

GAME DAY!

Vikings fans wear purple and gold. Many also wear Viking-themed gear. They wear hats with horns and long braids.

Viktor the Viking has been the team **mascot** since 2007. He helps fire up fans!

VIKTOR THE VIKING

BIG SHIP

A large model of the front of a Viking ship sits outside of U.S. Bank Stadium. Its sail is a large screen!

U.S. BANK STADIUM

A loud horn blows as the Vikings take the field. It also sounds after big plays. Fans cheer "Skol" at key moments. The song "Skol Vikings" plays when the Vikings do well.

Vikings fans love to cheer for their favorite team!

★ FAMOUS PLAYERS ★

FRAN TARKENTON

Quarterback

Played 1961–1966, 1972–1978

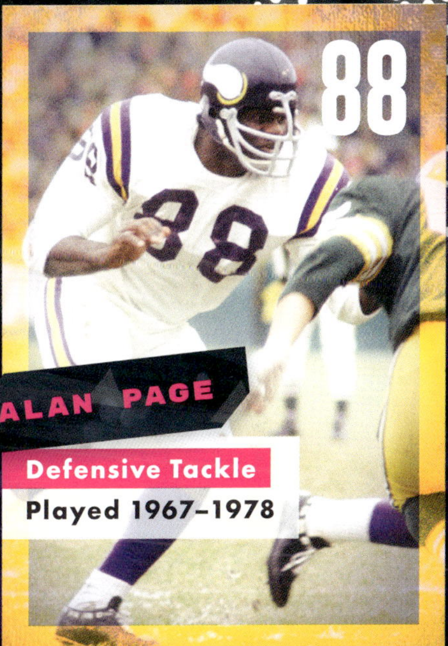

ALAN PAGE

Defensive Tackle

Played 1967–1978

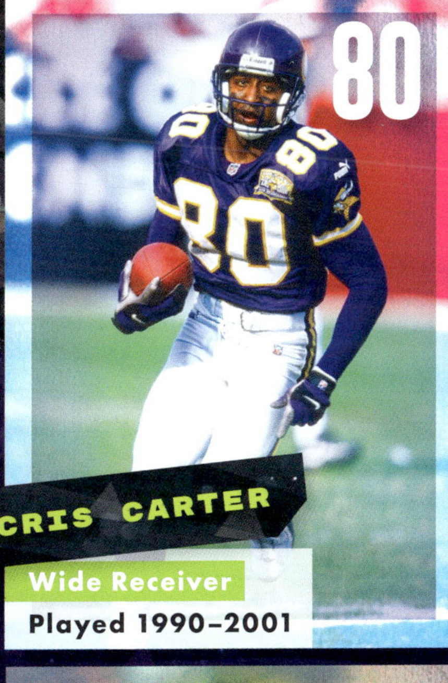

CRIS CARTER

Wide Receiver

Played 1990–2001

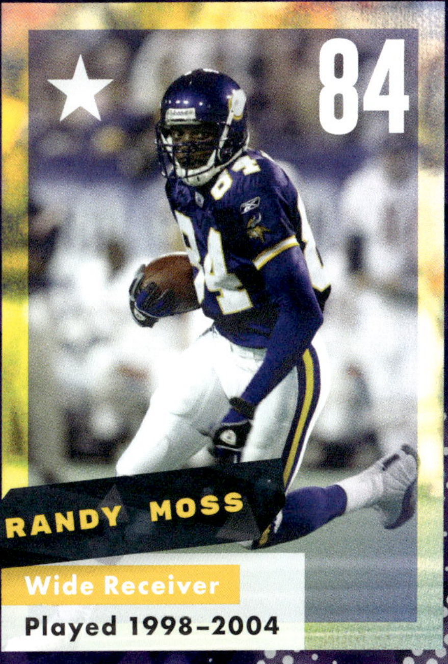

RANDY MOSS

Wide Receiver

Played 1998–2004

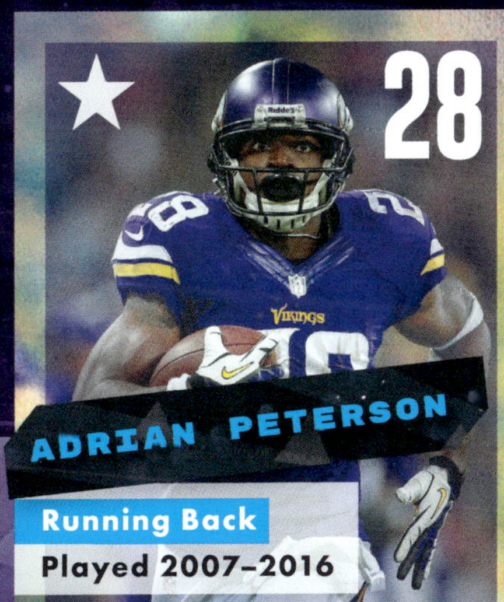

ADRIAN PETERSON

Running Back

Played 2007–2016

MINNESOTA VIKINGS FACTS

LOGO

JOINED THE NFL	1961
NICKNAME	The Purple and Gold

MASCOT

VIKTOR THE VIKING

CONFERENCE

National Football Conference (NFC)

COLORS

DIVISION | NFC North

Chicago Bears

Detroit Lions

Green Bay Packers

STADIUM

U.S. BANK STADIUM

opened July 22, 2016

holds around 66,000 people

TIMELINE

1961
The Vikings play their first season

1970
The Vikings play in their first Super Bowl

1999
The Vikings play in the NFC Championship Game

2018
The Vikings beat the Saints in the Minneapolis Miracle

2022
The Vikings win the NFC North for the fifth time

★ RECORDS ★

All-Time Passing Leader	All-Time Rushing Leader	All-Time Receiving Leader	All-Time Scoring Leader
Fran Tarkenton	Adrian Peterson	Cris Carter	Fred Cox
33,098 yards	11,747 yards	12,383 yards	1,365 points

GLOSSARY

championship—a contest to decide the best team or person

defensive tackle—a player whose main job is to tackle runners

division—a group of NFL teams from the same area that often play against each other; there are eight divisions in the NFL.

mascot—an animal or symbol that represents a sports team

offense—the group of players who have the ball and try to score

playoffs—games played after the regular season is over; playoff games determine which teams play in the championship game.

quarterback—a player whose main job is to throw and hand off the ball

rivals—long-standing opponents

stadium—an arena where sports are played

Super Bowl—the annual championship game of the NFL

wide receiver—a player whose main job is to catch passes from the quarterback

TO LEARN MORE

AT THE LIBRARY

Mitchell, Bo. *Justin Jefferson.* Mankato, Minn.: North Star Editions, 2023.

Ryan, Todd. *Minnesota Vikings.* Minneapolis, Minn.: Abdo Publishing, 2020.

Whiting, Jim. *The Story of the Minnesota Vikings.* Mankato, Minn.: The Creative Company, 2020.

ON THE WEB

FACTSURFER

Factsurfer.com gives you a safe, fun way to find more information.

1. Go to www.factsurfer.com.
2. Enter "Minnesota Vikings" into the search box and click 🔍.
3. Select your book cover to see a list of related content.

INDEX

The images in this book are reproduced through the courtesy of: Abbie Parr/ AP Images, cover; Scott Boehm/ AP Images, cover (stadium); David Berding/ Stringer/ Getty, p. 3; G. Newman Lowrance/ AP Images, p. 4; Hannah Foslien/ Stringer/ Getty, p. 5; Underwood Archives/ Contributor/ Getty, p. 6; Bettmann/ Contributor/ Getty, pp. 6-7, 8; Focus On Sport/ Contributor/ Getty, pp. 8 (inset), 9, 19 (Fran Tarkenton), 21 (1970, Fran Tarkenton, Fred Cox); Star Tribune via Getty Images/ Contributor/ Getty, p. 10; Abaca Press/ Alamy, p. 12; Isaiah Vazquez/ Stringer/ Getty, pp. 12-13; Icon Sportswire/ Contributor/ Getty, pp. 14, 16, 18-19; Mark Herreid, p. 15 (U.S. Bank Stadium); NFL/ Wikipedia, pp. 15 (Vikings logo), 20 (Vikings logo, Bears logo, Lions logo, Packers logo, NFC logo); Pinkcandy, pp. 16-17, 20 (stadium); David Durochik/ AP Images, p. 19 (Alan Page); Joe Robbins/ AP Images, p. 19 (Cris Carter); Tom Hauck/ Contributor/ Getty, p. 19 (Randy Moss); PhotoKrathy - Editorial/ Alamy, p. 19 (Adrian Peterson); Michael Steele/ Staff/ Getty, p. 20 (mascot); Tony Tomsic/ AP Images, p. 21 (1961); Matthew Stockman/ Staff/ Getty, p. 21 (1999); Jamie Squire/ Staff/ Getty, p. 21 (2018); Stephen Maturen/ Stringer/ Getty, pp. 21 (2022), 23; PA Images/ Alamy, p. 21 (Adrian Peterson); Joseph Patronite/ Contributor/ Getty, p. 21 (Cris Carter).